THE ARMY AND HOMELAND SECURITY: A STRATEGIC PERSPECTIVE

Antulio J. Echevarria II

March 2001

FOREWORD

The topic of homeland security includes a broad array of missions and mission areas ranging from national missile defense to military assistance to civil authorities. Recently the topic has attracted a great deal of attention due to the public's heightened awareness of the variety and nature of emerging threats and of the United States' vulnerabilities to them.

This monograph, written by Lieutenant Colonel Antulio J. Echevarria II, grew out of a tasking by the Army Staff to investigate the Army's role in homeland security from a strategic, rather than a legal or procedural perspective. The author achieves this perspective by placing homeland security missions within the larger spectrum of operations. In so doing, he exposes potential problem areas—missions requiring more or different force structure than that already available—for further action by the Army. He also recommends that the Army consider alternative force-sizing metrics that include, as a minimum, the "high-end" homeland security identified in the study.

DOUGLAS C. LOVELACE, JR.
Director
Strategic Studies Institute

BIOGRAPHICAL SKETCH OF THE AUTHOR

ANTULIO J. ECHEVARRIA II is a lieutenant colonel in the U.S. Army currently assigned as the Director of Strategic Research at the Strategic Studies Institute at Carlisle Barracks, PA. He graduated from the U.S. Military Academy in 1981, was commissioned as an armor officer, and has held a variety of command and staff assignments in Germany and Continental United States; he has also served as an assistant professor of European history at the U.S. Military Academy; Squadron S3 of 3/16 Cavalry; Chief of BN/TF and Bde Doctrine at the U.S. Army Armor Center at Fort Knox; as an action officer at the Army After Next project at HQ TRADOC, Ft. Monroe, VA; and as a speechwriter for two U.S. Army Chiefs of Staff. He is a graduate of the U.S. Army's Command and General Staff College, and holds M.A. and Ph.D. degrees in History from Princeton University. He has published articles in a number of scholarly and professional journals to include the *Journal of Military History*, *War in History*, *War & Society*, *the Journal of Strategic Studies*, *Parameters*, *Joint Force Quarterly*, *Military Review*, and *Airpower Journal*. His book, *After Clausewitz: German Military Thinkers before the Great War*, was published by the University Press of Kansas in March 2001.

THE ARMY AND HOMELAND SECURITY: A STRATEGIC PERSPECTIVE

Throughout our nation's history, the U.S. Army and its sister Services have readily responded to the Constitutional requirement "to insure domestic Tranquility and provide for the common defence."[1] That requirement has obliged U.S. forces to conduct a broad range of missions from the suppression of sedition, as in the Whiskey Rebellion of 1794, to the reconquest of U.S. territories, as in the Second World War. However, global economic changes, the rapid advance of information technologies, and the increasing proliferation of long-range missiles and weapons of mass destruction (WMD) recently have added new dimensions to the requirement to protect the homeland.[2] Accordingly, political and military leaders have begun to voice concerns about America's growing vulnerability and what should be done about it.[3] It is both timely and appropriate, therefore, for the U.S. Army to reexamine the issue of homeland defense and to assess whether it possesses the necessary resources to perform its homeland security (HLS) missions while carrying out its other responsibilities under the national security and national military strategies.

This monograph approaches homeland security as a strategic issue, examining the Army's capacity to accomplish its HLS missions under the *current* force-sizing metric and war planning requirement to fight two simultaneous (or nearly simultaneous) major theater wars (MTWs).[4] Little agreement exists over whether the Services have sufficient forces to execute two MTWs even without the additional—and still difficult to quantify—requirements associated with HLS.[5] Furthermore, despite much debate about the future of U.S. national security strategy and much rhetoric about the vulnerabilities of the homeland, little of the work done to date on alternative strategies actually addresses the requirement to protect the homeland.[6] To assist the Department of Defense (DoD) in identifying requirements and assigning priorities for HLS, the Army should establish a force-sizing metric for its HLS missions, particularly its high-end missions (defined later).

Assumptions.

This monograph makes two fundamental assumptions. First, the United States will remain engaged in the world for the foreseeable future. As a result, its national security strategy of "Engagement" and its national military strategy of "Shape, Respond, Prepare Now" will remain unchanged in principle, even if the terms and priorities are altered.[7]

Second, if U.S. national culture and historical traditions are any indication, Americans will demand a domestic environment in which their homeland is secure, but civil authority and liberties remain intact and security measures are transparent.[8] Accordingly, the U.S. military will perform the bulk of its HLS missions as the supporting rather than the lead federal agency and may have to comply with fairly restrictive rules of engagement.[9]

A New Threat Environment.

With the ending of the Cold War and the emergence of a new technological revolution, the threat environment has changed. A number of regional powers, states of concern, and transnational groups already possess limited, if asymmetric, means capable of challenging the interests of the United States abroad and those of its allies.[10] Intelligence estimates indicate, for instance, that ballistic missiles will continue to proliferate over the next few decades. More than 25 countries currently possess ballistic missiles, though only two, Russia and China, have intercontinental ballistic missiles (ICBMs) capable of reaching the United States. However, China's missile arsenal will probably increase significantly in the next decade. Furthermore, as the report of the Commission to Assess the Ballistic Missile Threat to the United States (the

Rumsfeld report) concluded, within 5 years North Korea and Iran (and Iraq in 10 years) will have the capability to target the United States with ICBMs armed with conventional and unconventional warheads.[11] Conceivably, by 2010, any one of these states and a score of others could issue a "stay at home or else" ultimatum to the U.S. National Command Authority (NCA), thereby effectively threatening the nation's ability to protect its interests overseas.[12]

In addition, cruise missiles—which vary in type from relatively inexpensive unmanned aerial vehicles (UAVs) to million-dollar-per-copy Tomahawks—have proliferated enormously in recent years. Approximately 19 nations currently produce cruise missiles of some type, while more than 75 countries possess them. Often referred to as the "poor-man's air force," cruise missiles are much cheaper to develop and easier to conceal than ballistic missiles. They can also carry payloads similar to those of ballistic missiles, but can deliver them with greater effectiveness because of their ability to make multiple passes. Intelligence estimates project a market of some 7,000 cruise missiles of the land-attack type by 2010, not counting Chinese or American purchases.[13] These missiles can be concealed in and launched from standard shipping containers. U.S. ports typically handle 13,000,000 shipping containers annually, but only a fraction of these are inspected. On any given day, about 1,000 ships travel the Atlantic Ocean, making it difficult to determine which vessel (or vessels) might launch, or had launched, a cruise missile against a U.S. target.[14] To date, the major sea and air ports of the United States lie virtually unprotected from an attack by land-or sea-launched cruise missiles.

Furthermore, assessments conducted by the United States Commission on National Security/21st Century (Hart-Rudman Commission) and the National Commission on Terrorism (Bremer Commission) point out that America remains vulnerable to a large-scale terrorist attack.[15] While the total number of terrorist incidents in the United States has declined from a high of 51 in 1982 to a low of 3 in 1996, the overall lethality of terrorism worldwide has risen from an average of 1,200 casualties during 1987-94 to more than 3,500 during 1995-97.[16] Intelligence projections, such as *Global Trends 2015*, suggest that this trend will continue.[17] What's more, some political leaders have expressed concern that large-scale domestic terrorism has already begun—as evidenced by the Oklahoma City bombing—and that extremist organizations like the Order and the Aryan Resistance are planning more attacks.[18] Domestic terrorism thus poses at least as serious a threat to U.S. citizens as the international brand, perhaps more.

Moreover, international and domestic terrorists appear to have grown more radical in their aims and methods. During the Cold War, international terrorists typically executed limited attacks so as not to undermine external political and financial support for their causes. Today, however, a number of international and domestic terrorist organizations seem motivated by revenge or apocalyptic fears, and seem bent on inflicting as many casualties as possible. Some international terrorists, such as Osama bin Laden and his al-Quaida organization, have achieved a considerable degree of fiscal and political independence and are thus less concerned that mass-casualty attacks would alienate their supporters. Hence, terrorist attacks in general have expanded in scale, as evidenced by the 1993 bombing of the World Trade Center, which was expected to yield some 60,000 casualties. Consequently, while the total number of terrorist incidents worldwide has declined over the years, intelligence estimates indicate that the overall likelihood of a terrorist attack in the United States involving a WMD has actually increased.[19]

Additionally, nuclear, biological, and chemical weapons have proliferated despite Congress' Cooperative Threat Reduction program with Russia, and the presence of such arms control regimes as the Chemical Weapons Convention (CWC) and Biological Weapons Convention (BWC).[20] Russia's inability to maintain accurate accountability of all of its WMD remains a source of concern; and Iran, Iraq, Libya, and North Korea, among others, continue to increase their chemical and biological stockpiles despite, in some cases, being signatories to one or both of these conventions. A WMD attack, whether delivered overtly by missiles or covertly by other means, could result not only in massive casualties, disruption or degradation of information infrastructures, contamination of public health systems and foodstuffs, and degraded response capabilities, but also in economic damage, loss of strategic world position, social-psychological damage, and undesirable political change.[21]

Finally, one must consider the potential menace to U.S. information systems posed by cyber attacks. The number of documented computer intrusion events has increased from 1,334 in all of 1993 to 8,800 in the first 6 months of 2000.[22] The Computer Security Institute estimates that computer crime in the United States doubled in 1999, causing nearly $10B in financial losses.[23] Because the sectors of the critical infrastructure of the United States—information and communications, vital human services, energy, physical distribution networks (e.g., waterways, bridges), and banking and finance—are becoming increasingly tied together electronically, cyber attacks can have a devastating effect on them as well. The Presidential Commission on Critical Infrastructure Protection assessed the vital human services and information and communications sectors as highly vulnerable to computer attack. The energy, physical distribution, and banking and finance sectors were classified as either well-protected or relatively resilient to an attack.[24] Nonetheless, as the Director of the Central Intelligence Agency testified before Congress in February 2000, the foreign cyber threat continues to grow. More than one dozen countries, including Russia and the People's Republic of China, have developed or are developing the means to launch strategic-level cyber attacks.[25]

Today's threat environment reflects the influences of a faster-paced and more interconnected world. In this environment, the traditional notion that "a threat = capabilities x intentions" remains valid, but requires more emphasis on potential threats than previously. Few of those states or nonstate actors that might wish to do the United States harm currently possess the capability to do so. Yet, even a slight increase in the rate of proliferation of long-range missile technologies and WMD means that our adversaries can acquire that capability sooner than we expect, perhaps sooner than we can implement countermeasures. In addition, computer "glitches" such as the Y2K bug possess no intent at all, but can nonetheless undermine national security when they become active. Accordingly, policymakers must now focus as much on possibilities as on probabilities, as much on vulnerabilities as on threats. Put differently, an effective homeland defense might require treating vulnerabilities as seriously as confirmed threats under the traditional reckoning.[26]

Definition of HLS and Mission Areas.

The U.S. Government needs to develop a comprehensive definition of HLS to provide a uniform basis for coordinating the efforts of all federal agencies and for deriving mission areas, tasks, and responsibilities for each. Remarkably, however, HLS has not yet been authoritatively defined, either at the interagency level or by the defense community.[27] Part of the reason for this is the disagreement over whether the definition should address only the requirement to "deter and defend against foreign and domestic threats" or whether it should encompass "all hazards," including natural and man-made disasters. Some views, such as those offered by RAND Arroyo, favor the former—a more circumscribed definition—because it provides a clear distinction between "military activities" and the "activities of civilian organizations."[28] They argue that such distinctions will reduce damage to the military's image, which could suffer harm if it is perceived as doing either too little or too much. Unfortunately, definitional clarity will not necessarily preclude misperceptions of whether the military has actually done too little or too much in any particular HLS situation. Furthermore, a circumscribed definition tends to make the problem fit the tools available; and would thus not help expose potential organizational or procedural weaknesses in the ways the U.S. Government and the Joint community propose to protect the homeland.

In the absence of an authoritative definition, the Army has rightly developed and tentatively approved the following "all-hazards" definition in its *HLS: Strategic Planning Guidance* (Draft dated Jan. 8, 2001):

> Protecting our territory, population, and infrastructure at home by deterring, defending against, and mitigating the effects of all threats to US sovereignty; supporting civil authorities in crisis and consequence management; and helping to ensure the availability, integrity, survivability, and adequacy of critical national assets.

Such a definition avoids dividing national security into "domestic" and "overseas" concerns and thereby helps preserve unity of effort in the execution of the national security and national military strategies. Second, it assists in reducing the potentially disruptive impact of an incident in which it is not clear whether hostile intent is involved by enabling the creation of a single chain of command appropriate for either situation. Finally, it facilitates the establishment of priorities and the allocation of resources.

This definition supports the following missions or mission areas described in the draft HLS *Strategic Planning Guidance*:

• *Land Defense*. The Army objective under Land Defense is to be prepared to participate as part of the joint force executing plans for the defense of the United States and its territories.

• *Responding to Chemical, Biological, Radiological, Nuclear, and High-yield Explosive (CBRNE) Incidents.* The Army objective in responding to CBRNE incidents is to organize, equip, and train units to timely, effectively and efficiently support the Lead Federal Agency in its efforts to: (1) reduce the vulnerabilities to CBRNE incidents; and (2) manage the consequences of CBRNE incidents.

• *National Missile Defense (NMD).* In the near-to-mid term the Army's objective is to perform those actions necessary to ensure the successful testing, deployment and operation of a land-based NMD system. The purpose of the NMD system as currently envisioned is to provide protection against limited ballistic missile attacks targeted at the United States. This protection will be achieved through integration of the NMD system elements with Integrated Tactical Warning and Attack Assessment (ITW/AA). The Army's Operational Concept for NMD can be found in TRADOC PAM 525-82.

• *Combatting Terrorism.* The Army objective under Combatting Terrorism is to provide training, staffing and equipment resources and services to support domestic emergencies consistent with national security priorities, Federal Response Plan criteria, and U.S. Code dealing with employment of military forces within the United States.

• *Critical Infrastructure Protection (CIP).* Protecting and defending critical infrastructure, including information and information systems. Army support will likely consist of equipment and forces to prevent the loss of, or to assist in restoring, telecommunications, electric power, gas and oil, banking and finance, transportation, water, emergency services, and government continuity. The Army objective under CIP is to develop a capability to ensure the availability, integrity, survivability, and adequacy of those assets deemed critical to the United States.

• *Information Operations (IO).* The Army objective under IO is to provide information operations in support of HLS efforts. Information operations are defined as defensive and offensive operations taken to affect adversary information and information systems while defending one's own information and information systems. While there are situations where a retaliatory IO offensive strike directed at an external entity might be undertaken to stop an ongoing attack, the general expectation is that HLS IO missions will be defensive in nature.

• *Military Assistance to Civil Authorities (MACA).* The Army objective under MACA is to provide essential support, services, assets, or specialized resources to help civil authorities deal with situations beyond their capabilities. MACA includes all of the actions that can be taken under the disaster-related Military Support to Civil Authorities (MSCA).

As this list reveals, the Army's HLS missions span a broad spectrum. In addition, they take place in parallel with other activities reflected in the Army's Spectrum of Operations. As Figure 1 illustrates, the Army's HLS missions correspond to low- and high-end operations based on their frequency and magnitude. For example, Environmental Operations, which are often high in frequency but low in magnitude, correspond with the left or low-end of the spectrum. Last year's fire-fighting activities in the northwestern United States were significant events for the soldiers involved, but those activities did not tax the Army's (or DoD's) resources to the degree that a WMD attack would have.

By contrast, operations at the right end of the spectrum tend to occur less frequently, if at all, but demand more resources, and often of a specific kind. The exception to this rule is Domestic Relief, which can occur anywhere along the spectrum depending upon the size of the incident. As a general rule, then, those incidents with the lowest probability of occurrence could result in the most severe consequences and, accordingly, would require the greatest amount of resources.

Figure 1.

It is doubtful that most low-end HLS missions would prevent the Army from executing a two-MTW scenario. However, it is almost certain that some high-end HLS missions would. A WMD incident, for example, could require sufficient resources to halt or interrupt the flow of forces from the continental United States (CONUS) and thereby seriously affect the commander-in-chiefs' (CINCs) war plans. Since defense officials currently assess the risk to U.S. forces as "moderate" for the first MTW and "high" for the second, any disruptions in the flow of forces would compound an already acute strategic dilemma.

As a minimum, therefore, the Army should develop a HLS force-sizing metric for its high-end missions, specifically its WMD and NMD missions (and possibly Domestic Relief, though it is not clear under what circumstances it would cause the NCA to halt the flow of forces overseas). Moreover, the process of developing such a metric would help the Army (and the defense establishment at large) to refine the full range of potential HLS missions, develop planning factors, assess requirements, identify areas of possible conflict between HLS and warfighting missions, and determine how to develop a force to fit the metric.[29]

A Force-sizing Metric for HLS.

WMD. It is difficult to forecast with precision the number and type of resources a WMD incident would require. The variables involved are too numerous and diverse for hard-and-fast rules. Planners at Joint Forces Command Task Force for Civil Support (JTF-CS) have nonetheless used the best information available from the Defense Threat Reduction Agency (DTRA) to develop draft "playbooks" that offer an estimate of the resources required to respond to three possible high-end events: the detonation of a 10KT nuclear device; a persistent chemical strike; or the discharge of a high-yield explosive device.[30]

By these estimates, the resources required to respond to the detonation of a 10KT nuclear device include: four (light) infantry battalions; five medical companies; three chemical battalions; three engineer construction battalions; three military police companies; four ground transportation battalions; an aviation group; three direct support maintenance battalions; and two general support maintenance battalions. Resources required to respond to a persistent chemical strike or to an incident involving the detonation of high-yield explosives would amount to some 30 percent of those required for a 10KT nuclear event. While these numbers might appear small, it is important to remember that the loss of even a single medical, chemical, or signal element can render larger units non-mission capable for the prosecution of an MTW.

Naturally, a combination of incidents would require more resources. However, that amount might not equal the simple sum of resources required for each incident. A combination of incidents could well produce a negative synergy that would require more resources. Yet, it might also result in a reduced resource demand overall depending upon the timing and proximity of the events.

Since an infinite number of scenarios are possible, the Army requires a force-sizing metric that balances resources and requirements within acceptable risk parameters. The Probability-Severity Matrix included as Figure 2 represents one possible framework for such a force-sizing metric. Cross-indexing the probability of an event with its anticipated severity produces a Probability-Severity Index (SI) that can also serve as a resource baseline. For instance, an SI equal to one 10KT incident (the detonation of a nuclear device the size of a 55 gallon drum) reflects probability of occurrence that is greater than that of a 15KT incident, but lower in severity.

The Army might, for example, consider establishing a force-sizing metric capable of addressing an SI of 2x10KT events, which would accommodate any number of scenarios in which one or two nuclear devices are brought into the United States covertly. A scenario involving three or more devices suggests that the perpetrators have access to considerable resources—not only weapons but also means of transportation and concealment—and that they have planned a well-coordinated assault. In such a case, the United States would probably be engaged in a war for national survival in which "all bets are off" and the National Command Authority would likely direct all resources against the perpetrators, assuming they could be identified. In addition, a resource baseline capable of addressing 2x10KT events would enable the Army to respond to several incidents, such as a 1x15KT or 1x22KT incident, or approximately 3x1KT nuclear incidents, or three biological or chemical attacks.[31]

NMD. Ideally, NMD would include a robust, multi-layered defensive system consisting of space, air, sea, and land weapons capable of long-range—strategic—defense as well as shorter-range—theater—defense. Although it seems clear that the United States will erect some form of NMD, support for it is far from unanimous, for technical and political reasons.

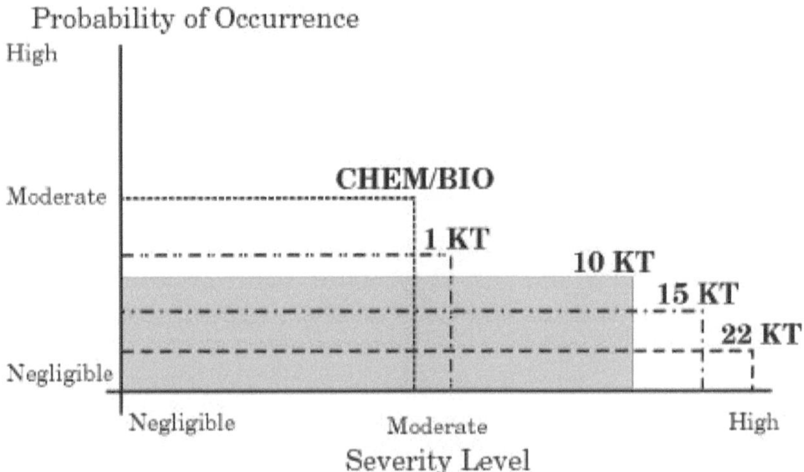

Figure 2.

The technical argument, presented by such outspoken critics as Dr. Theodore Postol, is that the technology does not exist (and probably never will) to enable an interceptor to distinguish a real missile from the chaff or decoys that inevitably accompany it. However, experts at the U.S. Space and Missile Defense Command have successfully refuted this argument by showing that Postol's claims pertained to an obsolete version of interceptor technology.[32]

The political argument for not building an NMD, proffered most conspicuously by Russia and China, is that implementation will cause an expensive and dangerous arms race, or have an otherwise destabilizing influence worldwide.[33] However, this is a specious argument. An arms race is essentially already underway as evidenced by the proliferation of missile technology. An NMD, which is a defensive system, not an offensive one, and presumably can be extended to our friends and allies, serves as a necessary counterweight to the dangers inherent in proliferation. In a manner of speaking, it represents a "threat" primarily to those states inclined to use their offensive missile capabilities to threaten others. Rather than exerting a destabilizing influence, in fact, NMD could contribute to maintaining or restoring peace and stability by precluding a "state of concern" from using its ballistic missiles to deter the United States or its allies from intervening in a regional crisis.

Another component of NMD is a shorter-range antimissile system capable of defeating cruise missiles. Such a system would also meet some requirements for force protection as well as the defense of critical infrastructure. The type and number of systems required would naturally depend upon a careful analysis of such factors as mission, enemy, troops, terrain, and time (METT-T). Excluding the understandable desire to provide an anti-missile shield over every major U.S. port or city, the defense of only critical ports and airfields along the east, west, and Gulf coasts, and the Great Lakes would still require a large number of systems. For example, some 147 Nike-Ajax and Nike-Hercules air-defense sites were constructed in the United States during the Cold War.[34]

To be sure, the Army's force-sizing metric will also have to include the other HLS mission areas. However, those most likely to have an impact on the force structure necessary for the U.S. military to execute 2MTWs are WMD and NMD.

Developing a HLS Force.

Once the Army has developed a force-sizing metric for HLS, it will need to examine the options available for filling that metric. Two of the more popular options are described below:

1. Add HLS as a "third MTW" to the current two-MTW force-sizing metric and assign high-end missions to an appropriate number of Army National Guard (ARNG) divisions (along with full-time soldiers as necessary).

2. Convert the current two-MTW force-sizing metric into one overseas MTW (or multiple smaller-scale contingencies) and one within CONUS for HLS missions.

Option 1 has the advantage of maintaining a larger force for deterring aggression or, if necessary, for defeating an adversary quickly and decisively. It also retains more forces for executing smaller-scale contingencies abroad—which many strategists claim will characterize the strategic environment for the foreseeable future—and reducing the excessively high operational tempo for the Army overall. In addition, it reduces the risk that unforeseen crises would draw units away from transformation. Furthermore, the stability that most ARNG units enjoy would enable their personnel to become well-established in their communities and develop critical working relationships with local law enforcement, fire departments, paramedics, and other emergency response organizations. (In many cases, ARNG and Reserve personnel are also local "first-responders" and that could pose a challenge unless planned for beforehand.) Such relationships can aid communications efforts among responding authorities and help reduce the inevitable fog and friction that would attend a major incident.[35]

However, reequipping an appropriate number of full-time ARNG divisions for WMD response and missile defense of the homeland will require substantial additional funds. The Army would also have to de-conflict any warfighting missions that might already have been assigned to some of those units.

Option 2 comes in a variety of forms. Fundamentally, it has much in common with any option—such as focusing on smaller-scale contingencies—that calls for scaling back the number of MTWs the U.S. armed forces must address, or eliminating them altogether. Overall, this option has the advantage of directing more resources toward HLS without increasing the total amount of defense spending. It is possible that this option would even allow for further reductions in force structure, thereby freeing funds for redirection to other federal agencies so as to increase border security, drug interdiction activities, and critical infrastructure protection.

However, it has significant disadvantages in that it reduces U.S. influence overseas, as well as U.S. ability to deter war or to fight more than one major conflict at a time. This option would require changing U.S. strategy to "win-hold-win" and thus would mean placing more emphasis on (and ultimately more funding in) Halt-phase operations to stop an aggressor's advance in one theater while a friendly counteroffensive takes place in another. Yet, as the results of the Kosovo campaign indicate, one-dimensional operations—which currently characterize the Halt-phase concept—entail a high degree of risk and tend to produce ambiguous results. In short, option 2 trades flexibility in crisis response for better protection at home.[36]

In sum, each option would cause defense planners and strategists to address HLS and national security as a single, integrated activity. Each would also place the desired emphasis on HLS missions. However, only option 1 permits the United States to address high-end HLS missions while retaining its present capability to deter war and to fight and win two conflicts simultaneously.

At the same time, this comparison illustrates that the two-MTW force-sizing metric has *outlived its usefulness*.[37] The two-MTW metric fails to capture, for example, the requirements for HLS, not to mention those associated with other missions, such as peacetime engagement. The Army should consider whether another metric would enable it to quantify and communicate its force structure requirements more accurately.

Clearly, HLS requirements must be imbedded in whatever overall force-sizing metric is chosen. In any case, the major conclusion of this monograph—that the Army needs to develop a HLS force-sizing metric—remains valid even if the overall two-MTW force-sizing metric is changed.

Recommendations.

In summary, this monograph recommends that the Army do the following:

- Consider alternative force-sizing metrics that include high-end HLS missions as a minimum;

- Advocate development of an NMD system to include defense against cruise missiles;

- Continue to emphasize the importance of HLS in the development of national security and national military strategies.

Whether and to what extent the United States is attacked in the future will depend a great deal upon how its potential adversaries perceive the measures taken to defend it. If prudent steps have been taken, fewer opportunities will exist for harm, and the United States will find itself in a better position to mitigate the effects of harm should it occur.

ENDNOTES

1. For a summary of the Army's contribution to the "common defence," see Gregory J. W. Urwin, "The Army of the Constitution: The Historical Context," in Max G. Manwaring (ed.), ". . . *to insure domestic Tranquility, provide for the common defence. . .*" Carlisle, PA: Strategic Studies Institute, 2000, pp. 27-62.

2. For the purposes of this monograph, WMD refers to chemical, biological, nuclear, radiological, and high-yield explosives as well as those generally referred to as weapons of mass effect (WME), such as electro-magnetic pulse or computer viruses. The term "weapons of mass destruction" is controversial. Mike Osterholm and John Schwartz, *Living Terrors: What America Needs to Know to Survive the Coming Bio-terrorist Catastrophe* (New York: Delacorte Press, 2000) point out that the term conveys the sense that defense against such weapons is

primarily a military or police concern rather than one affecting all citizens.

3. Phillip A. Odeen, *et al., Transforming Defense: National Security in the 21st Century* (Arlington, VA: National Defense Panel, December 1997), was one of the first documents to raise homeland defense as a strategic concern.

4. While recent indications are that the 2MTW force-sizing metric will soon change, this monograph resulted from a tasking to investigate homeland security within the context of 2MTWs. For indications that the Joint community is considering abandoning the 2MTW metric, see Elaine M. Grossman, "Military Makeover: Fight two wars at once? That's old thinking," *Boston Globe*, January 7, 2001, p. D1.

5. Many analysts, in fact, maintain that not only does the U.S. military lack the forces for a 2MTW scenario, but the force-sizing metric itself is antiquated and does not reflect the full range of today's strategic requirements. See Steven Metz, ed., *Revising the Two MTW Force Shaping Paradigm*, Carlisle, PA: Strategic Studies Institute, Forthcoming, 2001.

6. An example of such a discussion is Michael O'Hanlon, "Rethinking Two War Strategies," *Joint Force Quarterly*, Spring 2000, pp. 11-17, which proposes an additional 10 percent cut in U.S. armed forces, but fails to mention homeland defense. Such omissions are due in part to DoD's position that it will play a supporting role in homeland defense and its failure to define better the full range of HLS missions and their potential overlap with warfighting missions—a deficiency addressed in the recommendations of Michèle A. Flournoy, *Quadrennial Defense Review 2001 Working Group*, Washington, DC: National Defense University, November 2000, p. 60. Nonetheless, a vast amount of material on HLS issues does exist. See, for example, the recent publications on homeland defense by the Center for Strategic and International Studies and the *Journal of Homeland Defense (www.homelanddefense.org)* .

7. Public pronouncements by key members of the new administration suggest that the United States will remain engaged in the world. See, for example, the speech of Dr. Condoleeza Rice, the Bush administration's National Security Advisor, at the Fletcher Conference, November 15, 2000; and Condoleeza Rice, "Promoting the National Interest," and Robert B. Zoellick, "A Republican Foreign Policy," *Foreign Affairs*, January/February 2000, pp. 45-62, 63-78, here 45 and 70, respectively.

8. In a speech to the National Academy of Sciences on January 22, 1998, President Clinton assured the public that those demands would be met, declaring that even in the face of a growing bioterrorist threat, the government would remain committed to upholding "privacy rights and other constitutional protections, as well as the proprietary rights of American businesses."

9. Thomas R. Lujan, "Legal Aspects of Domestic Employment of the Army," *Parameters*, Vol. 27, No. 3, Autumn 1997, pp. 82-97, offers an excellent summary of legal lessons learned from selected domestic employments of the Army during the 1990s.

10. A useful summary of key aspects of the U.S. homeland and their vulnerabilities to asymmetric attack is provided in Kenneth F. McKenzie, Jr., *The Revenge of the Melians: Asymmetric Threats and the Next QDR*, McNair Paper No. 62, Institute for National Strategic Studies, November 2000, pp. 60-64, Table 7. *Global Trends 2015: A Dialogue about the Future* (*http://www.cia.gov/cia/publications/globaltrends2015)* states that asymmetric approaches will become the "dominant characteristic" of most threats to the U.S. homeland.

11. Donald H. Rumsfeld, *et al.*, *The Report of the Commission to Assess the Ballistic Missile Threat to the United States*, Washington, DC, July 15, 1998, pp. 8-9.

12. Institute for Foreign Policy Analysis, *Exploring U.S. Missile Defense Requirements in 2010,* Washington, DC: IFPA, April 1997, p. 6-9.

13. *Cruise Missile Threats*; and *Emerging Cruise Missile Capabilities*, Center for Defense and International Security Studies, *http://www.cdiss.org/cmthreat.htm*; *Ballistic and Cruise Missile Threats*, National Air Intelligence Center, NAIC-1031-0985-98, *http://www.fas.org/irp/threat/missile/tabled.htm*. The Institute for Foreign Policy Analysis, *Assessing the Cruise Missile Puzzle: How Great a Defense Challenge?* (Washington, DC: IFPA, November 2000), p. 3, reports that 80,000 cruise missiles comprised of 75 different types are deployed in 81 different countries.

14. *http://www.ceip.org/programs/npp/cruise4.htm*.

15. The United States Commission on National Security/21st Century, *Seeking a National Strategy: A Concert for Preserving Security and Promoting Freedom*, April 15, 2000; and the Report of the National Commission on Terrorism, *Countering the Changing Threat of International Terrorism*, The Terrorism Research Center, June 7, 2000.

Some critics maintain, however, that as dramatic as terrorist attacks are, "to call them a serious threat to national security is scarcely plausible." John and Karl Mueller, "Sanctions of Mass Destruction," *Foreign Affairs*, Vol. 78, No. 3, May/June 1999, pp. 43-53. This view is successfully rebutted by Patrick L. Moore, "Is Catastrophic Terrorism Just Strategic 'Peanuts?'" *National Security Law Report*, Vol. 22, No. 4, July-August 2000, pp. 1, 5-6.

16. *Terrorism in the United States 1996,* Washington, DC: FBI, *http://www.ncvc.org/stats/dt.htm;* and *Anti-US Attacks, 1987-97*, Director of Central Intelligence, Counterterrorist Center, *http://www.cia/di/products/terrorism/attacks.gif*; and *Total Casualties Worldwide, 1987-1997* (graph), *http://www.cia/di/products/terrorism/worldwide.gif*.

17. *Global Trends 2015, http://www.cia.gov/cia/publications/globaltrends2015.*

18. Hon. John Train, "Who Will Attack America?' *Strategic Review,* Fall 2000, pp. 11-15.

19. *Global Trends 2015.* Amy E. Smithson and Leslie Anne Levy, *Ataxia*, Stimson Center Report No. 35, contend that terrorist use of BW and CW will remain difficult. See also Bruce Hoffman, "Terrorism by Weapons of Mass Destruction: A Reassessment of the Threat," in *Transnational Threats: Blending Law Enforcement and Military Strategies*, Carolyn W. Pumphrey, ed., Carlisle, PA: Strategic Studies Institute, November 2000, pp. 85-104. Hoffman essentially argues that terrorists cannot overcome the difficulties of employing WMD, and so will not use them. His argument is successfully defeated by Victor Utgoff, "Bruce Hoffman's View of Terrorism by Weapons of Mass Destruction: Another Perspective," pp. 133-136, in the same volume. See also Walter Laquer, *The New Terrorism*, New York: Oxford, 1999.

20. Richard Latter, "Chemical and Biological Weapons: Forging a Response to a Twenty-first Century Threat," Wilton Park Paper, October 2000, points out that, while 139 states have signed the CWC and 27 of 61 declared CW production facilities have been destroyed thus far, concerns remain over clandestine programs and the absence of Middle Eastern and North-east Asian states as signatories. Similarly, the BWC is hampered by the absence of any arrangements to verify compliance. On the need to bolster CW and BW arms control regimes, see: Jonathan B. Tucker and Kathleen M. Vogel, "Preventing the Proliferation of Chemical and Biological Weapon Materials and Know-How," *The Nonproliferation Review*, Vol. 7, No. 1, Spring 2000, pp. 88-96, esp. 95; Marie I. Chevier, "Strengthening the International

Arms Control Regime," in *Biological Warfare: Modern Offense and Defense*, Raymond A. Zilinskas, ed., Boulder: Lynne Reinner, 2000, pp. 149-176; and Laurie Garrett, "The Nightmare of Bioterrorism," *Foreign Affairs*, January/February 2001, pp. 76-89.

21. Much depends upon the social and historical context of the attack. *The Landmark Thucydides: A Comprehensive Guide to the Peloponnesian War,* Robert B. Strassler, ed., (New York: Simon & Schuster, 1998); and Giovanni Boccaccio, *The Decameron*, Jonathan Usher, trans., (New York: Oxford University Press, 1998), provide examples of how an epidemic can cause political and social chaos. However, the great flu epidemic of 1918, devastating as it was, caused no such disruption. Gina Kolata, *Flu: The Story of the Great Influenza Pandemic of 1918 and the Search for the Virus that Caused it* (New York: Touchstone, 2001). Henry W. Fischer III, *Response to Disaster: Fact Versus Fiction & Its Perpetuation*, 2d ed., (New York: University Press of America, 1998), indicates that chaos will be a typical organizational response, but not for individuals, provided they are kept well-informed.

22. Computer Emergency Response Team (CERT) Coordination Center, *www.cert.org/stats/cert_stats.html*.

23. Charles Piller, "Cyber-Crime Loss at Firms Doubles to $10 Billion," *Los Angeles Times*, March 22, 2000; cited from F. G. Hoffman, *Homeland Defense: A Net Assessment*, Washington, DC: Center for Strategic and Budgetary Assessments, Forthcoming 2001.

24. Robert T. Marsh, *Critical Foundations: Protecting America's Infrastructure*, Washington, DC: President's Commission on Critical Infrastructure Protection, October 1997, pp. 11-20, Appendix A.

25. Hoffman, *Homeland Defense*.

26. For supporting views on the need to change the traditional definition of a threat, see Colonel Randall J. Larsen, U.S. Air Force (Retired) and Ruth A. David, "Homeland Defense: Assumptions First, Strategy Second," *Strategic Review*, Fall 2000, pp. 4-10; and Phillip E. Lacombe, "Daniel T. Kuehl's View of DOD's Role in Defending the National Information Infrastructure: Another Perspective," in *Transnational Threats*, pp. 163-172.

27. Ashton B. Carter, "Keeping America's Military Edge," *Foreign Affairs* (January/February 2001), pp. 90-105, esp. 94, in fact, lists homeland defense as one of the "homeless missions" that are accomplished in an "ad-hoc fashion by unwieldy combinations of

departments and agencies designed a half-century ago for a different world."

28. Eric V. Larson and John E. Peters, DRAFT, *The Army Role in Homeland Defense: Concepts, Issues and Options*, RAND Arroyo Center, October 1999, pp. vi-xvii.

29. See *Quadrennial Defense Review 2001*, p. 60, for similar points cast as recommendations.

30. Playbooks for other scenarios are under development, but have not yet progressed to the draft stage.

31. The baseline of 2x10KT also accords roughly with a RAND draft study, October 1999, that proposed planning guides of one 22KT nuclear incident of 100,000 casualties, three chemical attacks of 5,000 casualties each, and three biological attacks of 10,000 casualties each.

32. Lieutenant General John Costello, Commander USASMDC, briefing presented at the Annual U.S. Army Space and Missile Defense Command Conference, August 22, 2000. Dr. Postol was invited, but declined to participate in the conference. See also The Institute for Foreign Policy Analysis, *National Missile Defense: Policy Issues and Technical Capabilities*, July 2000, Final Edition. Nonetheless, criticism of developing an NMD continues; see "Missile Shield Illusions," *New York Times*, on the web, January 10, 2001.

33. There are also issues with the 1972 ABM Treaty that remain to be resolved. R. James Woolsey, "The Way to Missile Defense: Dealing with Russia and Ourselves," *National Security Law Report*, Vol. 22, No. 3, May-June 2000, pp. 1-2, 5-6, provides a brief discussion of the provisions of the ABM Treaty and suggests how it might be changed. He also discusses a cheaper alternative that would employ satellites.

34. *http://www.zianet.com/dpiland/ordnance/wspg.htm.*

35. The advantages and disadvantages of using Army Reserve (and by extension some ARNG forces) in a HLS role are discussed in Charles L. Mercier Jr., "Terroists, WMD, and the US Army Reserve," *Parameters,* Vol. 27, No. 3, Autumn, 1997, pp. 98-118.

36. On the limited efficacy of air operations in the Kosovo campaign, see Admiral Bill Owens, *Lifting the Fog of War,* New York: Farrar, Straus, & Giroux, 2000, pp. 181-183. For a critique of the Halt-phase concept, see Earl H. Tilford, Jr., *Halt Phase Strategy: New Wine in Old Skins . . . with Powerpoint*, Carlisle, PA: Strategic Studies Institute, 1998.

37. For a discussion of force-sizing alternatives, see Metz, *Revising the Two MTW Force Shaping Paradigm.*

U.S. ARMY WAR COLLEGE

Major General Robert R. Ivany
Commandant

*****

STRATEGIC STUDIES INSTITUTE

Director
Professor Douglas C. Lovelace, Jr.

Director of Research
Dr. Earl H. Tilford, Jr.

Author
Lieutenant Colonel Antulio J. Echevarria II

Director of Publications and Production
Ms. Marianne P. Cowling

Publications Assistant
Ms. Rita A. Rummel

*****

Composition
Mrs. Christine A. Williams

Cover Artist
Mr. James E. Kistler

www.ingramcontent.com/pod-product-compliance
Ingram Content Group UK Ltd.
Pitfield, Milton Keynes, MK11 3LW, UK
UKHW041901190726
13854UKWH00003B/1007

9 781312 379848